QUICK-WORD®

Handbook for Beginning Writers

animal	earth	head	one
away	eat	hear	only
back	eyes	is	op
big	face		
body	far		
can	feel		
clean	feet		
close	fin		
color			
come	go		
could	gone		s
day	great	m	upon
does	ground	near	want
ear	grow	noise	young

This handbook belongs to

Curriculum Associates®

TABLE OF CONTENTS

FOR THE STUDENT

The **QUICK-WORD® Handbook for Beginning Writers** contains the basic 330 high-use words that new writers need. Each word is introduced along with a sentence that uses the word in context. Each sentence is made from the basic words only. The sentence helps the student establish both the meaning of the word and the use of the word in a sentence. Space is also provided for beginning writers to add their own important words. Eight special pages appear at the back of the handbook. These pages feature related words that are also useful to new writers.

For more advanced writers, the authors suggest using The **QUICK-WORD® Handbook for Everyday Writers**, which contains 1,220 high-use writing words. To order this handbook, ask for catalog number 132.

Get the most out of this handbook!
Download your free copy of Ten Terrific Tips at www.CurriculumAssociates.com/QW-Beginning

The original **QUICK-WORD® Handbook for Beginning Writers** was prepared by Rebecca A. Sitton and Robert G. Forest, Ed.D. This updated version was compiled by Robert G. Forest.

Illustrations by Leslie Alfred
Cover photograph: ©2010 JupiterImages Corporation

ISBN 978-0-7609-4080-8
©2010, 2007, 2002, 1992—Curriculum Associates, LLC
North Billerica, MA 01862

My name

My city
or town

My state
or province

My school

My teacher

My Words

Word list	Sentences
a	We will walk <u>a</u> mile.
about	The book is <u>about</u> a king.
after	Night comes <u>after</u> day.
again	Say your name <u>again</u>.
all	I ate <u>all</u> my food.
am	I <u>am</u> near the house.
an	She has <u>an</u> idea.
and	You <u>and</u> I are friends.
animal	A cat is an <u>animal</u>.
any	Do you have <u>any</u> paper?
are	We <u>are</u> at school.
as	Run <u>as</u> fast <u>as</u> you can!
ask	Did you <u>ask</u> your mom?
at	Dad is <u>at</u> home.
ate	Who <u>ate</u> the food?
away	My sister went <u>away</u>.

alone

Bb

My Words

baby	The <u>baby</u> is so little.
back	Come <u>back</u> here!
ball	We should play <u>ball</u>.
be	Will you <u>be</u> there?
because	I ran <u>because</u> I was late.
bed	Is it time to go to <u>bed</u>?
been	I have <u>been</u> home all day.
between	Look <u>between</u> the lines.
big	The nest is <u>big</u>, not little.
body	The baby has a small <u>body</u>.
book	Read more than one <u>book</u>!
both	<u>Both</u> children will help us.
boy	He is a good <u>boy</u>.
build	Who will <u>build</u> our house?
but	Run fast, <u>but</u> don't fall.
by	Sit <u>by</u> me!

 Cc — My Words

call	I will <u>call</u> your name.
came	Mom <u>came</u> to school.
can	My brother <u>can</u> read.
can't	We <u>can't</u> see them. (cannot)
car	The <u>car</u> is near the road.
care	I <u>care</u> about you.
carry	Mother will <u>carry</u> the baby.
children	The <u>children</u> play ball.
city	I live in a big <u>city</u>.
clean	We must <u>clean</u> the yard.
close	Please <u>close</u> the door.
cold	The ice is always <u>cold</u>.
color	What <u>color</u> are your eyes?
come	<u>Come</u> here now!
could	We <u>could</u> help them.
cut	Who <u>cut</u> the grass?

Dd

day	Today is a cold <u>day</u>.
dear	You are a <u>dear</u> friend.
deep	The water is <u>deep</u>.
did	I <u>did</u> not need a chair.
didn't	He <u>didn't</u> go home. (did not)
do	What <u>do</u> you need?
does	How <u>does</u> this look?
done	Our job is <u>done</u>.
don't	<u>Don't</u> run! (do not)
door	Open the <u>door</u>.
down	I may fall <u>down</u>.
draw	We will <u>draw</u> a picture.
drink	You may <u>drink</u> the water.
drive	She can <u>drive</u> the car.
drop	Did you <u>drop</u> the plant?
dry	The paint is now <u>dry</u>.

each	Give one to <u>each</u> child!
ear	An <u>ear</u> can hear.
early	The children came <u>early</u>.
earth	The <u>earth</u> was very dry.
east	Our farm is <u>east</u> of the city.
easy	My job was <u>easy</u>.
eat	When will we <u>eat</u>?
else	What <u>else</u> do you know?
end	How does the story <u>end</u>?
enough	I have <u>enough</u> to do.
even	She didn't <u>even</u> see us.
ever	Did you <u>ever</u> find him?
every	Read <u>every</u> day!
everyone	<u>Everyone</u> is so happy.
everything	We saw <u>everything</u>.
eyes	Her <u>eyes</u> are beautiful.

My Words

Word list	Sentences
face	Your <u>face</u> is clean.
fall	The rain will soon <u>fall</u>.
family	My <u>family</u> lives here.
far	Keep everyone <u>far</u> back!
farm	We need help to run the <u>farm</u>.
father	My <u>father</u> is kind.
feel	Do you <u>feel</u> happy?
feet	My <u>feet</u> are large.
few	We have a <u>few</u> books.
find	Did you <u>find</u> the lost cat?
first	The girl can write her <u>first</u> name.
food	Did you eat your <u>food</u>?
for	We look <u>for</u> a quiet time.
found	I <u>found</u> an old car.
friend	Who is your best <u>friend</u>?
from	She comes <u>from</u> the city.

Gg

My Words

game	We will play a game.
gave	I gave her the kitten.
get	Get ready to go!
girl	That girl really is quiet.
give	Please give me the book!
go	Is it time to go home?
goes	She goes to school.
going	We are going to the zoo.
gone	Some people have gone.
good	The food was so good.
got	We got more rain.
grass	The grass grows fast.
great	We had a great time.
ground	Place the pot on the ground.
group	I have a group of friends.
grow	We grow plants.

 Hh — My Words

had	Everybody <u>had</u> a place to go.
hand	Give me your <u>hand</u>.
hard	The ice is <u>hard</u>.
has	Who <u>has</u> my key?
have	We <u>have</u> a new car.
he	<u>He</u> can't help us!
head	The cut was on my <u>head</u>.
hear	What do you <u>hear</u>?
help	They need your <u>help</u>.
her	<u>Her</u> mother is near.
here	<u>Here</u> we are.
him	We need <u>him</u> now!
his	What is <u>his</u> real name?
home	Please take the animal <u>home</u>.
house	I live in a new <u>house</u>.
how	<u>How</u> old do you think I am?

Ii

I	<u>I</u> like to read books.
ice	Put <u>ice</u> in the water.
I'd	<u>I'd</u> do it if I could.
idea	What is your <u>idea</u>?
if	Help me, <u>if</u> you can.
I'll	<u>I'll</u> see you soon. (I will)
I'm	<u>I'm</u> so happy. (I am)
in	We ran <u>in</u> the yard.
inch	The line is one <u>inch</u> long.
into	Did he go <u>into</u> the house?
is	Who <u>is</u> your friend?
isn't	The door <u>isn't</u> open. (is not)
it	Give <u>it</u> to me!
its	The animal plays with <u>its</u> feet.
it's	<u>It's</u> the real thing! (it is)
I've	<u>I've</u> been so good. (I have)

job	My <u>job</u> is often easy.
join	I may <u>join</u> your group.
joy	The children bring us <u>joy</u>.
jump	How far did you <u>jump</u>?
just	I'll use <u>just</u> one pan.
keep	<u>Keep</u> your head down!
kept	We <u>kept</u> enough food.
key	I found the car <u>key</u>.
kind	What <u>kind</u> do you want?
king	The <u>king</u> can't drive.
kitten	The <u>kitten</u> likes to jump.
knew	I <u>knew</u> they would come.
knife	Use a <u>knife</u> to cut the food.
know	We <u>know</u> where to look.
known	I've <u>known</u> him for a long time.

land	He will farm the <u>land</u>.
large	The zoo is very <u>large</u>.
last	Who is <u>last</u> in line?
late	I will not be <u>late</u>.
learn	What new idea did you <u>learn</u>?
leave	When did they <u>leave</u>?
let	<u>Let</u> everyone know!
letter	She did write the <u>letter</u>.
life	They hope for a long <u>life</u>.
like	We <u>like</u> to read.
line	Draw the <u>line</u> here!
little	The children are so <u>little</u>.
live	I <u>live</u> in this house.
long	The story is much too <u>long</u>.
look	<u>Look</u> at the picture.
low	Her voice is very <u>low</u>.

Mm

My Words

made	She <u>made</u> the bed.
make	I will <u>make</u> new friends.
man	He is a nice <u>man</u>.
many	We saw <u>many</u> people.
may	You <u>may</u> visit them.
me	Show <u>me</u> your picture.
mean	What does this <u>mean</u>?
men	The <u>men</u> are outside.
mile	He ran one <u>mile</u>.
more	How much <u>more</u> do you need?
most	Who has the <u>most</u> time?
mother	My <u>mother</u> likes everyone.
move	I could not <u>move</u> the rock.
much	How <u>much</u> paint did you use?
must	We <u>must</u> find our pet.
my	You are <u>my</u> friend.

name	What is your <u>name</u>?
near	Don't go <u>near</u> the water!
need	Do you <u>need</u> help?
never	<u>Never</u> run in the house!
new	I need a <u>new</u> job.
next	You are <u>next</u> in line.
night	I visit them every <u>night</u>.
no	There is <u>no</u> more room.
noise	Did you hear the <u>noise</u>?
noon	They will leave at <u>noon</u>.
north	Our house is <u>north</u> of the city.
not	I'm <u>not</u> cold.
note	Did you read my <u>note</u>?
nothing	We have <u>nothing</u> to do.
now	Must we go <u>now</u>?
number	A <u>number</u> of people were there.

Oo — My Words

of	Look in the back <u>of</u> the book.
off	Did he fall <u>off</u> the bed?
often	It <u>often</u> rains early in the day.
oh	<u>Oh</u>, what did you do?
old	Mother found an <u>old</u> book.
on	Who would draw <u>on</u> the wall?
once	<u>Once</u> is enough.
one	We saw <u>one</u> animal.
only	We <u>only</u> have this picture!
open	Is the door <u>open</u>?
or	Use this <u>or</u> that.
other	Go the <u>other</u> way.
our	<u>Our</u> school is large.
out	The children ran <u>out</u> the door.
over	Jump <u>over</u> the rock.
own	Does she <u>own</u> a car?

Pp

My Words

page	Color each <u>page</u>.
paint	We have enough <u>paint</u>.
pan	The <u>pan</u> is large.
paper	This book is made of <u>paper</u>.
part	Give me a <u>part</u> of it!
people	<u>People</u> live in the city.
pick	We must <u>pick</u> a new king.
picture	Draw a <u>picture</u>.
place	Find a quiet <u>place</u> to read.
plan	We <u>plan</u> to build here.
plant	A <u>plant</u> needs water.
play	Did you <u>play</u> the game?
point	<u>Point</u> to the picture you like.
pot	Is the <u>pot</u> full?
pull	<u>Pull</u> the string.
put	<u>Put</u> paint in the can.

Qq Rr — My Words

question	Ask me a <u>question</u>.
quick	The grass is <u>quick</u> to grow.
quiet	Please be <u>quiet</u>!
rain	How much <u>rain</u> will fall?
ran	The animal <u>ran</u> by us.
read	<u>Read</u> me a story.
ready	Are you <u>ready</u> to go?
real	The picture looks <u>real</u>.
really	I <u>really</u> like school.
ride	Did you <u>ride</u> in the car?
right	Look to the <u>right</u>.
road	The <u>road</u> is long.
rock	We found a large <u>rock</u>.
room	My bed is in this <u>room</u>.
round	The earth is <u>round</u>.
run	You must <u>run</u> fast!

 Ss

My Words

said	I <u>said</u> each name.
same	We had the <u>same</u> idea.
saw	I looked up and <u>saw</u> her.
say	What did you <u>say</u>?
school	We often draw in <u>school</u>.
see	<u>See</u> the happy children!
she	Is <u>she</u> a good queen?
should	You <u>should</u> always be ready!
show	<u>Show</u> me how to draw.
side	The key will open the <u>side</u> door.
small	The room is much too <u>small</u>.
so	I can go and <u>so</u> can you.
some	We need <u>some</u> more food.
still	I <u>still</u> can't see the road.
story	Mom may read us a <u>story</u>.
sun	The <u>sun</u> is high at noon.

take
tell
than
that
the
their
them
then
there
these
they
thing
think
this
time
to

Tt

My Words

Take your time.

What did you tell her?

A few is more than one.

I pick that picture.

See the girl and boy run.

Where is their house?

Give them the ball.

Go up and then go down.

My friend is over there.

I need these books.

What will they do?

Each thing is round.

Think about my idea.

I like this story.

Is it time for bed?

We should go to the zoo.

under	Look <u>under</u> the chair.
until	Wait <u>until</u> the rain is over.
up	Will she ever grow <u>up</u>?
upon	He jumps <u>upon</u> the bed.
us	Show <u>us</u> the way.
use	<u>Use</u> your head to think.
usually	We <u>usually</u> ride to school.
verb	Which word is a <u>verb</u>?
very	The food was <u>very</u> good.
village	We live in a small <u>village</u>.
visit	They <u>visit</u> us once a year.
voice	She has a nice <u>voice</u>.

want	I <u>want</u> to grow vegetables.
was	He <u>was</u> in bed all night.
water	Don't drink the <u>water</u>!
way	I know the <u>way</u> home.
we	<u>We</u> saw the kittens.
were	We <u>were</u> there last night.
what	<u>What</u> time is it?
when	<u>When</u> do we eat?
which	<u>Which</u> one do you want?
who	<u>Who</u> are you?
will	I <u>will</u> give you more room.
with	You must go <u>with</u> us.
word	I will spell this <u>word</u> correctly.
work	Where do you <u>work</u>?
would	What <u>would</u> you do?
write	Who will <u>write</u> the letter?

-Xx Yy Zz- My Words

yard	He may play in the <u>yard</u>.
year	The baby is one <u>year</u> old.
yell	I did hear a <u>yell</u>.
yes	<u>Yes</u>, I'll visit with you.
yesterday	Did it rain <u>yesterday</u>?
yet	Is it time to get up <u>yet</u>?
you	I gave <u>you</u> the right book.
you'll	<u>You'll</u> eat soon. (you will)
young	The children are so <u>young</u>.
your	Where is <u>your</u> friend?
you're	<u>You're</u> next. (you are)
yourself	Did you do it by <u>yourself</u>?
zoo	We saw the animal at the <u>zoo</u>.

Days of the Week

Sunday

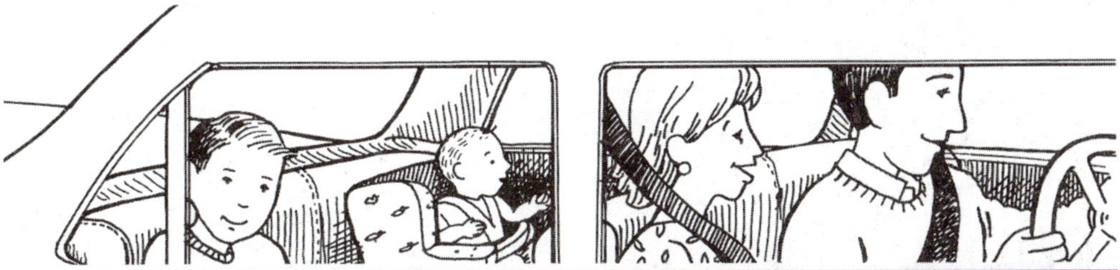

Monday

Tuesday

Wednesday

Thursday

Friday

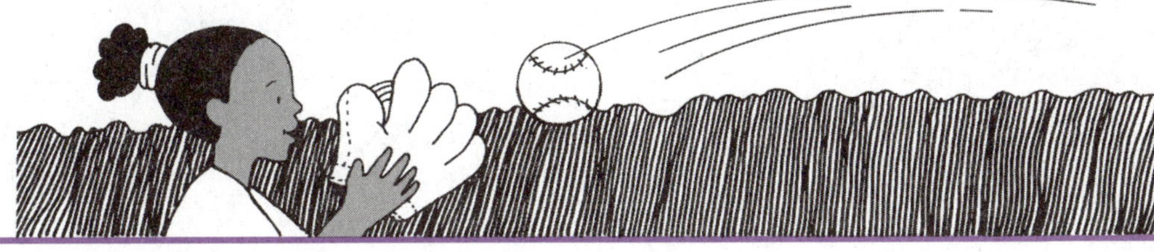

Saturday

Months of the Year

January
February
March

April
May
June

July
August
September

October
November
December

Weather Words

sunny 

The day is <u>sunny</u>.

rainy 

The day is <u>rainy</u>.

snowy 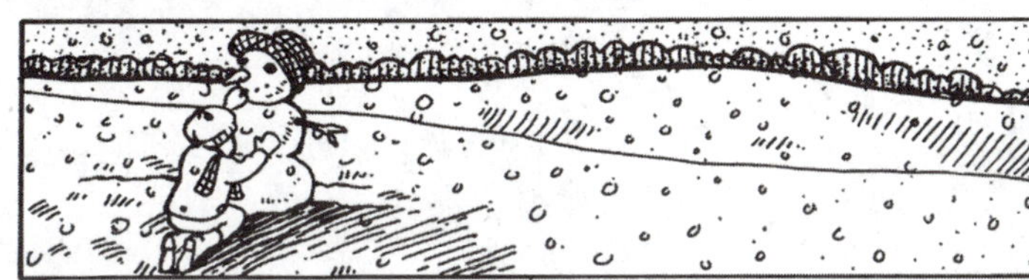

The day is <u>snowy</u>.

cloudy 

The day is <u>cloudy</u>.

windy 

The day is <u>windy</u>.

foggy 

The day is <u>foggy</u>.

cold 

The day is <u>cold</u>.

hot 

The day is <u>hot</u>.

Animals

bear	fish
bird	horse
cat	lion
chicken	monkey
cow	mouse
dog	pig
duck	sheep
elephant	squirrel

Foods

apple		ice cream	
banana		milk	
cake		orange	
cereal		pancakes	
cookies		pie	
eggs		pizza	
hamburger		sandwich	
hot dog		vegetables	

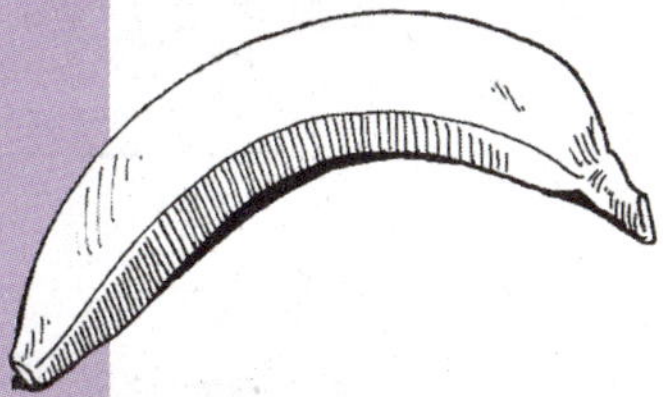

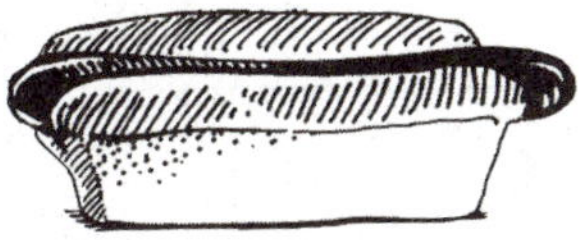

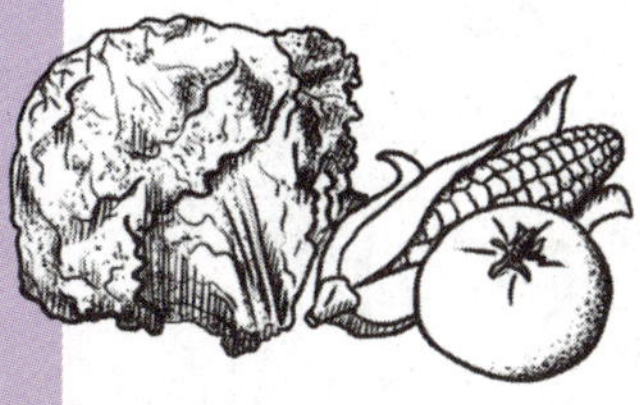

Color each.

red

blue

yellow

green

orange

purple

black

white

pink

gray

brown

School Words

book 

paper 

halk 

pencil 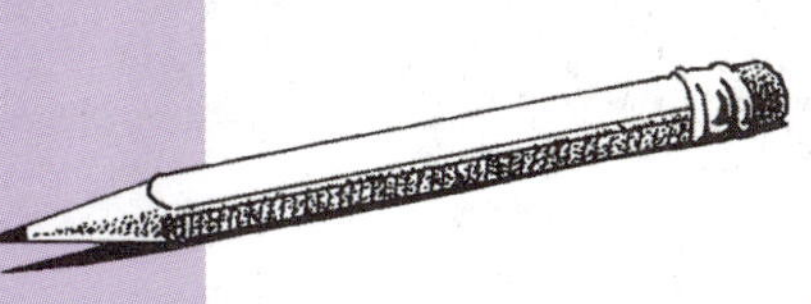

halkboard 

scissors 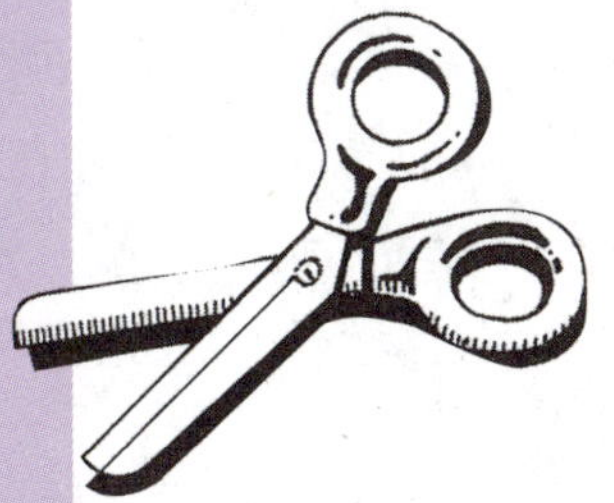

rayons 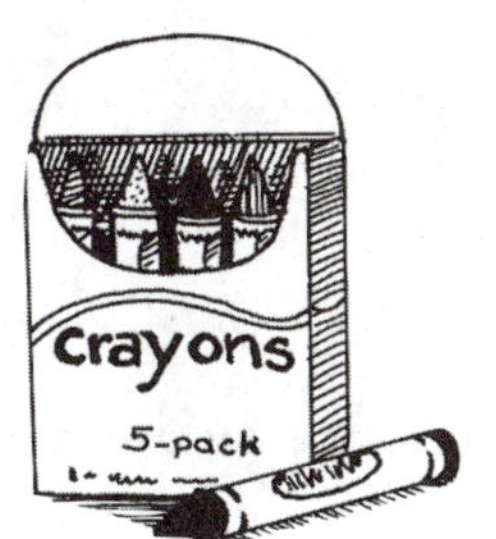

student 

raser 

table and
chair 

lue 

teacher 

Numbers

zero	0
one	1
two	2
three	3
four	4
five	5
six	6
seven	7
eight	8
nine	9
ten	10

Curriculum Associates®   800 225-0248   CurriculumAssociates.com   **Reorder No. CA10403—Single**